MW01242692

The Los Angeles Chargers Facts For Fan

Every Fan Of This Team Should To Know

Copyright © 2020

All rights reserved.

DEDICATION

The author and publisher have provided this e-book to you for your personal use only. You may not make this e-book publicly available in any way. Copyright infringement is against the law. If you believe the copy of this e-book you are reading infringes on the author's copyright, please notify the publisher at: https://us.macmillan.com/piracy

Contents

Introduction

The Los Angeles Chargers are a professional American football team based in the Los Angeles metropolitan area. The Chargers compete in the National Football League (NFL) as a member club of the league's American Football Conference (AFC) West division. The Chargers play their home games at SoFi Stadium in Inglewood, California, which the club shares with the Los Angeles Rams.

The club was founded as a Los Angeles-based team on August 14, 1959, and began play on September 10, 1960, as a charter member of the American Football League (AFL). They spent their first season in Los Angeles before relocating to San Diego in 1961 to become the San Diego Chargers. The Chargers joined the NFL as result of the AFL–NFL merger in 1970. The return of the Chargers to Los Angeles was announced for the 2017 season, just one year after the Rams had moved back to the city from St. Louis. They have previously played at the Los Angeles Memorial Coliseum during their first stint in Los Angeles, Balboa Stadium and Qualcomm Stadium while in San Diego and Dignity Health Sports Park, formerly named StubHub Center, from 2017 to 2019 while SoFi Stadium was under construction.

The Chargers won one AFL title in 1963 and reached the AFL playoffs five times and the AFL Championship four times before joining the NFL (1970) as part of the AFL–NFL merger. In the 43 years since then, the Chargers have made 13 trips to the playoffs and four appearances in the AFC Championship game. In 1994, the Chargers won their lone AFC championship and faced the San Francisco 49ers in Super Bowl XXIX, losing 49–26. The Chargers have eight players and one coach enshrined in the Pro Football Hall of Fame in Canton,

Ohio: wide receiver Lance Alworth (1962–1970), defensive end Fred Dean (1975–1981), quarterback Dan Fouts (1973–1987), head coach–general manager Sid Gillman (1960–1969, 1971), wide receiver Charlie Joiner (1976–1986), offensive lineman Ron Mix (1960–1969), tight end Kellen Winslow (1979–1987), linebacker Junior Seau (1990–2002), and running back LaDainian Tomlinson (2001–2009).

History of the Los Angeles Chargers

The Los Angeles Chargers are a professional American football team that currently plays and competes in the National Football League (NFL). The Chargers were established in 1960 and played one season in Los Angeles before moving to San Diego in 1961. The team returned to Los Angeles in 2017.

Beginnings: The 1960 AFL Season

The Los Angeles Chargers were established with seven other American Football League teams in 1959. In 1960, the Chargers began AFL play in Los Angeles. The Chargers' original owner was hotel heir Barron Hilton, son of Hilton Hotels founder Conrad Hilton.

According to the official website of the Pro Football Hall of Fame, Barron Hilton agreed after his general manager, Frank Leahy, picked the Chargers name when he purchased an AFL franchise for Los Angeles: "I liked it because they were yelling 'charge' and sounding the bugle at Dodgers Stadium and at USC games." The Chargers initially considered playing at the Rose Bowl, but instead signed a lease to play at the Los Angeles Coliseum.

Los Angeles Chargers 1960 wordmark

In 1960, the Chargers began AFL play in Los Angeles; both Barron Hilton and Conrad Hilton unveiled the Chargers' uniforms which featured blue and gold with lightning bolts on the sides of the helmets and trousers, at a cocktail party at Hilton's Santa Monica residence. Players Jack Kemp and Ron Mix modeled the new uniforms. On the

3

field, the Chargers overcame a 20–7 deficit in the fourth quarter to defeat the Dallas Texans 21–20 before 17,724 persons in the L.A. Coliseum in the opening league game. A crowd of 9,928 in the L.A. Coliseum watched the Chargers top the Denver Broncos 41–33 to clinch the AFL Western Division title. American Broadcasting Company (ABC) held the television rights and televised key games. On January 1, a crowd of 32,183 in Jeppesen Stadium and a national television audience saw host the Houston Oilers defeat the Chargers 24–16 in the AFL championship game.

San Diego Era

The Chargers only spent one season in Los Angeles before moving to San Diego in 1961. Initially denied in December, 1960, but announced in late January, 1961, owner Barron Hilton relocated the Chargers down the coast to a soon-to-be expanded Balboa Stadium at Balboa Park in San Diego for the 1961 season, their home field until 1966. In August 1967, they moved to the newly constructed San Diego Stadium (later renamed Jack Murphy Stadium, then Qualcomm Stadium), where they played their home games until 2016.

The Chargers won their only AFL Championship when they defeated the Boston Patriots in the 1963 AFL Championship Game. After the 1970 merger with the NFL, the team made their lone Super Bowl appearance in 1994, a loss to the San Francisco 49ers in Super Bowl XXIX.

Carson Stadium Plan

By the late 2000s, Qualcomm Stadium, one of the last remaining venues in the league to have been built as a multi-purpose stadium, was becoming obsolete. Potential independent stadium projects intended to lure a team to Los Angeles targeted the Chargers as one of several teams that could potentially relocate to Los Angeles. The Chargers were seen as a potentially favorable candidate, given their history in Southern California, the ease in which they could opt out of their current stadium deal, and owner Alex Spanos's advanced age and senility (raising the possibility that son and heir apparent Dean Spanos could be willing to sell a portion of the team in the event of his father's death). The Chargers, during this time frame, publicly committed to stay in San Diego each year and rejected the offers of other stadium developers.

In 2014, the Chargers, the St. Louis Rams, and the Oakland Raiders all intimated they might apply for relocation to Los Angeles at the end of the season. The Chargers announced in December 2014 that they would not be seeking to relocate for the 2015 season, followed by an announcement from the NFL that no team would relocate to L.A. until the 2016 season at the earliest.

In 2015, team spokesperson Mark Fabiani continued to bash the local San Diego city government's efforts to negotiate a replacement for Qualcomm Stadium. When the St. Louis Rams owner Stan Kroenke announced in January 2015 his intention to build a new stadium in Inglewood, California, the Chargers felt pressured to announce their own Los Angeles plan to preserve what they claimed was "25 percent of their fan base" in the affluent Los Angeles and Orange County areas. In February 2015, the team announced a stadium proposal in Carson, California, in partnership with the Oakland Raiders, their AFC West divisional rivals.

The day following the conclusion of the 2015 regular season, the Chargers, Rams, and Raiders all filed to relocate to Los Angeles. On January 12, 2016, the NFL owners voted 30–2 to allow the Rams to return to Los Angeles and approved the Inglewood stadium project over the Carson project. The Chargers were given a one-year approval to relocate, conditioned on negotiating a lease agreement with the Rams or an agreement to partner with the Rams on the new stadium construction.

On January 14, 2016, the team filed paperwork for official trademark protection of the term "Los Angeles Chargers" for the purposes of running and marketing a professional football franchise. Later in January, the Chargers submitted to the City of Santa Ana grading and landscape plans for a five-acre parcel of land in the city that could be used as the location of interim headquarters and training facilities "in the event the team exercises its option to relocate to the Los Angeles area." After two weeks of negotiation, the Chargers and Rams came to an agreement in principle on sharing the planned SoFi Stadium on January 29, 2016. The Chargers would contribute a $200 million stadium loan from the NFL and personal seat license fees to the construction costs and would pay $1 per year in rent to the Rams.

As an incentive to work out a stadium deal in their current market, the NFL pledged $100 million to the Chargers if they come to an agreement with the city of San Diego. While the team had until March 2016 to decide if they would relocate to Los Angeles for the 2016 season, Chargers chairman/CEO Dean Spanos announced on January 29, 2016, that the team would remain in San Diego for the season. The announcement stated that the team would also be working over the year with government and business leaders on a new stadium proposal that could keep the team in San Diego long-term.

The Chargers had continued preliminary work on a ballot initiative for public approval on a new facility. On February 23, 2016, the Chargers announced that their stadium efforts would be focused on a stadium in East Village, Downtown San Diego. On March 30, 2016, it was reported in the media that the details of the downtown stadium proposal were unveiled the stadium would be financed from $650 million from the team and the NFL, with a tax hike of $1.15 billion in bonds including $350 million city contribution, $600 million for the convention center, and $200 million to acquire land. On April 21, 2016, rendering of the proposed downtown stadium were unveiled by the Chargers and on April 23, 2016, the downtown stadium initiative signature collecting was launched with Roger Goodell, Philip Rivers, LaDainian Tomlinson, Mike McCoy, and Dean Spanos. On June 10, 2016, the Chargers announced that they had collected 110,786 signatures for the downtown stadium initiative 1 month later on July 9, 2016, San Diego City Clerk Liz Malland announced that the downtown Chargers stadium initiative had secured enough valid signatures to be put on the November 2016 ballot. On July 18, 2016, the San Diego City Council voted 8–0 to put the Chargers stadium plan and the Citizens Plan on the November ballot. On July 28, 2016, the San Diego Regional Chamber of Commerce announced its support of the Chargers downtown stadium proposal. On October 3, 2016, Mayor Kevin Faulconer officially announced his support of the Chargers stadium plan. On November 8, 2016, Measure C was voted down (57% opposed over 43% in support). On December 14, 2016, at an owners' meeting, the terms of the Chargers and Rams lease agreement, as well as the team's debt ceiling were approved thus taking the first steps for a possible relocation to Los Angeles in 2017. On December 23, 2016, the Chargers agreed to lease part of a Costa Mesa office campus for offices, practice fields, and training facility on nearly 3.2 acres.

Return to Los Angeles

Dignity Health Sports Park

Dignity Health Sports Park in Carson, where the Chargers played from 2017 to 2019

On January 12, 2017, Chargers chairman Dean Spanos announced in a letter that the team would be moving back to Los Angeles in time for the 2017 NFL Season. The Chargers also announced the team would play their games at the StubHub Center (now Dignity Health Sports Park) in Carson until the completion of Los Angeles Stadium at Hollywood Park (now known as SoFi Stadium) in 2020. There had been speculation that the team may rebrand itself similar to how the Houston Oilers ultimately became the Tennessee Titans in 1999. Unlike the situation between the Cleveland Browns and Baltimore Ravens, the Oilers' rebranding was done by the team's choice and not by court order. Plus, the Titans retained the franchise records of the

Oilers, unlike the Ravens who technically became a new franchise when they arrived from Cleveland in 1996. Arguments in favor of keeping the team's current name include the fact that team already had a history in Los Angeles (however distant and brief) and the presence of the team's existing fan base in the area on account of being the only Southern California-based franchise for more than two decades. The Chargers have announced they had no immediate plans to rebrand after the relocation, although a new alternate logo incorporating the letters "LA" with a lightning bolt was unveiled with the relocation announcement and quickly scrapped after it was "widely ridiculed".

Reaction to the relocation was not without controversy. Los Angeles Times columnist Bill Plaschke welcomed the team to town by writing "We. Don't. Want. You." At a game at the Staples Center between the Los Angeles Clippers and Lakers, the Chargers' regular logo was shown on a scoreboard and was "booed heartily" Chargers tight end Jeff Cumberland was also "jeered" by the crowd when featured on the big screen.

Anthony Lynn era

New beginnings

On January 13, 2017, the Chargers fired defensive coordinator John Pagano, replacing him with former Jaguars head coach Gus Bradley. The Chargers also announced they had hired Anthony Lynn to be their next head coach.

The Chargers narrowly missed the playoffs in 2017, losing out on a four-way tiebreaker with the Titans, Bills, and Ravens. In 2018, the Chargers finished the season 12–4 and went to the playoffs for the first time since 2013, making it to the divisional round before being eliminated by the eventual Super Bowl champions New England Patriots. Following a 5–11 finish in 2019, the Chargers allowed longtime quarterback Philip Rivers, who had started every game for the franchise since 2006, to walk in free agency, leaving backup Tyrod Taylor and 2020 first-round pick Justin Herbert to compete for the starting quarterback position.

List of Los Angeles Chargers seasons

The Los Angeles Chargers are a professional American football franchise based in the Greater Los Angeles Area. The Chargers compete in the National Football League (NFL) as a member club of the league's American Football Conference (AFC) West division. The club was founded in 1959 by Barron Hilton and played the 1960 season in Los Angeles as part of the American Football League (AFL). In the next season, the Chargers moved to San Diego. In 2017, the Chargers relocated back to the Los Angeles area.

The franchise has experienced three major periods of success. The first was from 1960 to 1965, when the Chargers were AFL West champions five times and AFL champions once. The second was from 1978 to 1982, when the Chargers had winning seasons (seasons with more wins than losses) in each of these years, and won three consecutive division championships for the second time in franchise history. The most recent accomplishments range from 2004 to 2009, with the franchise reaching the playoffs five times in six years. Their only Super Bowl appearance was in 1994.

The Chargers have experienced three notable periods of decline. Between 1970 and 1977, the Chargers never won more games than they lost as part of a 13-year period without playing in the postseason, including four consecutive years last in their division from 1972 to 1975, in which year they bottomed out before two late wins avoided the NFL's first 0–14 season. From 1983 to 1991, they never placed higher than third in their division and did not make the playoffs. From

1996 to 2003, the team had no winning seasons, and had their worst season ever, winning only one of 16 games in 2000.

The Chargers have been division champions nine times including 2009, all of them in the AFC West. They have been conference champions six times, but only once since the AFL-NFL merger in 1970. As of the end of the 2017 season, the Chargers had played 917 regular and post-season games in 58 seasons, and have appeared in the post-season seventeen times

Logos and uniforms

The Chargers' first logo, 1960; Alternate logo, 2018–present

Except for color changes along the way, the Chargers have essentially used the logo of an arc-shaped lightning bolt since the team debuted in 1960. During its period in the AFL, the club also used a shield logo that featured a horsehead, a lightning bolt, and the word "Chargers". The team brought the logo back for on-field design in the 2018 season.

From 1960 to 1973, the colors consisted of various shades of Electric blue ("powder" blue, but technically called Collegiate blue) or white jerseys, both with gold lightning bolts on the shoulders. The helmets were white and had both the arc-shaped lightning bolt logo, in gold or navy depending on the year, and the player's number. At first, the team wore white pants before switching to gold in 1966. In 1973, the numerals on the blue jerseys changed from white to gold.

In 1974, the sky blue was changed to dark royal blue. The helmet was also changed to dark blue and the players' numbers were removed. Additionally, the face masks became yellow, thus making them one of the first teams in the NFL (with the Kansas City Chiefs) to use a facemask color other than the then-predominant grey. From 1978 through 1983, the Chargers wore their white jerseys at home, coinciding with the hiring of coach Don Coryell – when Joe Gibbs, a Coryell assistant in 1979–80, became head coach of the Washington Redskins in 1981, he did the same, and white at home became a

Redskins staple through 2007 – but Coryell switched the Chargers to their blue jerseys at home starting in 1984. With the exception of the 1991 season and other sporadic home games since, San Diego wears its blue jerseys at home.

In 1985, the Chargers started using navy blue jerseys and returned to wearing white pants. The team's uniform design was next revamped in 1988. It featured an even darker shade of navy blue. The lightning bolts on the jerseys and helmets were white, with navy interior trim and gold outlining; the facemasks became navy blue. In 1990, the team started to wear navy pants with their white jerseys. From 1988 to 1991, the team displayed stripes down the pants rather than lightning bolts. The Chargers went with all-white combinations in 1997 and 2001, only to have the blue pants make a comeback. On October 27, 2003, the Chargers wore their navy pants with their navy jersey for a Monday Night Football game versus the Miami Dolphins that was played at Sun Devil Stadium, then the home of the Arizona Cardinals, due to wildfires in southern California. This remains the only game in which the Chargers have worn the all-dark combination.

From the late 1980s to 2000, the Chargers wore white at home during some preseason games and dark for regular season games. In 2001, the Chargers started wearing their dark uniforms for preseason games and white uniforms in September home games due to the heat before switching back to dark in October.

In March 2007, the Chargers unveiled their first uniform redesign since 1988, on the team's official website. The team formally unveiled this new uniform set, which mixes old and new styles, in a private team-only event. Navy blue remains the primary color on the home jersey, but the familiar lightning bolt was reverted to gold, and now has navy outlining and powder blue interior trim. The latter color is a nod to the 1960s uniforms. The redesigned lightning bolt was moved to the sides of the shoulders from the top, and includes a new numbering font and word mark in white, with gold outlining and powder blue interior trim. The pants also have a redesigned lightning bolt in gold, with powder blue trim on a navy stripe. Additionally, the team pays tribute to other uniform features from their history by wearing a metallic white helmet, with a navy face mask, the newly revamped bolt in gold with navy and powder blue trim, and white pants. The road white jerseys with navy pants, as well as the alternate powder blue jerseys with white pants, were also redesigned with the new scheme.

From 2002 to 2006, the Chargers used the early-1960s powder blue uniforms as alternate jerseys, which many football fans (both of the Chargers and of other teams) clamored for the team to bring back full-time.

Since 2007, the Chargers have worn the alternate powder blue jerseys twice per season. The alternate powder blue jerseys have also been worn in a playoff game against the Indianapolis Colts in 2008.

In 2009, in honor of their 50th anniversary as one of the eight original AFL teams, the Chargers wore their 1963 throwback uniforms for three games.

For the 2013 season, the Chargers made minor tweaks to their current uniforms. These include a two-tone nameplate (gold with powder blue trim on home jersey, navy with gold trim on away jersey, and white with navy trim on alternate jersey), collars matching the color of the jersey, and the addition of a gold stripe on the socks.

First Chargers wordmark of the second Los Angeles era 2017–2019

On January 12, 2017, with the announcement that the Chargers were moving to Los Angeles, the team unveiled a new alternate logo incorporating the letters "LA" with a lightning bolt. The logo was immediately and widely ridiculed by fans, the media, and even other professional sports franchises, in part for its resemblance to the Los Angeles Dodgers logo. The team tried to defuse the controversy by changing the color scheme of the new logo before scrapping it altogether after two days.

The team officially announced on April 16, 2019 that it would wear its powder blue jerseys, the same uniforms they wore during their inaugural season in 1960 while in Los Angeles, as its primary home uniform beginning with the 2019 NFL season. The club also announced that the facemask color would change from navy blue to gold, which was previously worn when the team wore its royal blue NFL Color Rush uniforms.

On March 24, 2020, the team announced new logos and upcoming new uniforms for the team. The new logos removed the navy blue completely, altered the double bolt lessening the curve, and debuted a new script logo featuring powder blue and gold and lightning bolt shooting from the A in Chargers. On April 21, 2020, the team unveiled their new uniforms. This uniform set has numbers on the helmet and includes two color-rush uniforms, a royal blue set similar to one the one used in their previous look, and an all-navy set, which has color of the logo on the helmet changed to navy as well. Gold pants were also included in the rebrand. Powder blue also returned as the primary color

Los Angeles Chargers retired numbers

The Los Angeles Chargers are a professional American football team in the National Football League (NFL) based in the Greater Los Angeles Area. The club began play in 1960 as a charter member of the American Football League (AFL), and spent its first season in Los Angeles before moving to San Diego in 1961. They returned to Los Angeles in 2017. NFL teams assign each of their players a jersey number ranging from 1 through 99. The Chargers no longer issue four retired numbers. As of 2010, the team's policy was to have the Chargers Hall of Fame committee evaluate candidates for a player's number to retire after the player has retired from the league after five years. The committee consisted of Chargers Executive Vice President A. G. Spanos, Chargers public relations director Bill Johnston, San Diego Hall of Champions founder Bob Breitbard, and the presidents of the San Diego Sports Commission and the Chargers Backers Fan Club. There are few recognized guidelines in sports regarding retiring numbers, and the NFL has no specific league policy. "You have to have enough numbers for players to wear," said NFL spokesman Greg Aiello. The Chargers have rarely retired numbers. The San Diego Union-Tribune wrote, "The tend to honor their heritage haphazardly."

Pro Football Hall of Fame offensive tackle Ron Mix in 1969 was the first Charger to have his number retired after he announced he was quitting football. However, he came out of retirement in 1971 to play for the Oakland Raiders. Then-Chargers owner Gene Klein, who hated the Raiders, unretired the number.

Dan Fouts had his No. 14 retired in 1988, a year after his retirement. He was the first NFL quarterback to top the 4,000-yard passing mark in three consecutive seasons. He set a then-NFL single-season passing record in 1981, throwing for a career-high 4,802 yards. At the retirement of his number, Fouts asked for "more recognition of former players and a warmer relationship between Charger players and management. I'd like to see Lance Alworth's number retired, too. We've had some great players here."

Alworth's No. 19 was retired in 2005, 35 years after he last played for the Chargers and 27 years after he was inducted into the Pro Football Hall of Fame. He was still one of the most popular athletes in San Diego history. Nicknamed Bambi for his speed and graceful leaping skills, Alworth was a pioneer for the Chargers and the AFL in the 1960s. He was selected All-AFL seven times from 1963–1969 and averaged more than 50 catches and 1,000 yards a year with San Diego. He retired with the most career yards (9,584) in team history, a record that held for almost 45 years.

The Union-Tribune in 2003 wrote that the Chargers no longer retired numbers, but Chargers president Dean Spanos said Junior Seau might be an exception. "If there's going to be another number retired, that's the one that's going to be retired," Spanos said. Seau made 12 consecutive Pro Bowl appearances with San Diego. He initially retired from the NFL in a 2006 ceremony with the Chargers, and the team planned to retire his number—as early as 2011—after his anticipated induction into the Pro Football Hall of Fame. However, Seau signed with the New England Patriots four days later, and continued playing until 2009. Seau's No. 55 was retired in 2012 posthumously at his memorial. "His play on the field combined with his leadership and charisma became the face of this team for more than a decade. I can't think of anyone more deserving of this honor," said Spanos.

After LaDainian Tomlinson signed a one-day contract and retired as a Charger in 2012, Dean Spanos said his number would be retired in the future. On November 22, 2015, the Chargers retired Tomlinson's No. 21.

Bob Wick, the Chargers equipment manager since 2000, said he tried to keep Charlie Joiner's No. 18 out of circulation, even though it has not been officially retired

Los Angeles Chargers Hall of Fame

Junior Seau honored at the Chargers Ring of Honor in San Diego

The Los Angeles Chargers are a professional American football team in the National Football League (NFL) based in the Los Angeles Area. The club began play in 1960 as a charter member of the American Football League (AFL), and spent its first season in Los Angeles before moving to San Diego in 1961. They returned to Los Angeles in 2017. The Chargers created their Hall of Fame in 1976. Eligible candidates for the Hall of Fame must have been retired for at least four seasons. Selections are made by a five-member committee chaired by Dean Spanos, Chargers vice-chairman. As of 1992, other committee members included Bob Breitbard, founder of the San Diego Hall of Champions; Ron Fowler, president of the Greater San Diego Sports Association; Jane Rappoport, president of the Charger Backers; and Bill Johnston, the team's director of public relations.

The initial four members—former players Emil Karas, Frank Buncom, Bob Laraba, and Jacque MacKinnon—were inducted posthumously in 1976. From 1986 through 1992, there were no new inductions. The Los Angeles Times wrote in 1992, "The Chargers have not done a good job in recent years of recognizing their former players." Dan Fouts and Charlie Joiner were inducted in 1993. "It embarrasses me to go into the Hall of Fame before Don Coryell, because if it wasn't for Don Coryell, I wouldn't be in the Hall of Fame for the Chargers," said Fouts of his former head coach. Coryell was inducted the following year. The Chargers allowed the 2012 inductee to be determined by fans, who selected punter Darren Bennett.

The members of the Hall of Fame were honored in San Diego at the Chargers Ring of Honor, founded in 2000 and viewable above the visiting team's sideline of Qualcomm Stadium on the press level. Before its introduction in 2000, the Chargers and the Oakland Raiders were the only NFL teams without a Ring of Honor. In 2013, the Chargers also inducted their 1963 AFL Championship team into their Ring of Honor; 15 members of the team were already in the team's Hall of Fame

List of Los Angeles Chargers head coaches

Don Coryell, head coach for the Chargers from 1978 to 1986, was famous for his "Air Coryell" offense.

The Los Angeles Chargers are a professional American football team based in the Greater Los Angeles Area. The Chargers compete in the National Football League (NFL) as a member club of the league's American Football Conference (AFC) West division. Their stadium is located in Inglewood, California. There have been 15 coaches in San Diego and Los Angeles franchise history, including Sid Gillman, who coached the Los Angeles Chargers' first and only season in 1960 before the team's move to San Diego, California in 1961. The current coach is Anthony Lynn, who replaced Mike McCoy in 2017.

History

This section may be too long and excessively detailed. Please consider summarizing the material while citing sources as needed. (April 2020)

Sid Gillman coached the Los Angeles and San Diego Chargers to five Western Division titles and one league championship in the first six years of the league's existence.

His greatest coaching success came after he was persuaded by Barron Hilton, then the Chargers' majority owner, to become the head coach of the American Football League franchise he planned to operate in

Los Angeles. When the team's general manager, Frank Leahy, became ill during the Chargers' founding season, Gillman took on additional responsibilities as general manager.

As the first coach of the Chargers, Gillman gave the team a personality that matched his own. Gillman's concepts formed the foundation of the so-called "West Coast offense" that pro football teams are still using. He coached the Los Angeles and San Diego Chargers to five Western Division titles and one league championship in the first six years of the league's existence.

He played college football at Ohio State University under legendary coach Francis "Shut the Gates of Mercy" Schmidt, forming the basis of his "West Coast offense." The term "West Coast Offense," as it is now commonly used, derives from a 1993 Bernie Kosar quote, publicized by Sports Illustrated writer Paul Zimmerman (or "Dr. Z"). Originally the term referred to the "Air Coryell" system used by two west coast teams beginning in the 1970s, the San Diego Chargers and Oakland Raiders. However, a reporter mistakenly applied Kosar's quote about the Air Coryell system to the 1980s-era attack of Walsh's San Francisco 49ers. Initially, Walsh resisted having the term misapplied to his own distinct system, but the moniker stuck. Now the term is also commonly used to refer to pass-offenses that may not be closely related to either the Air Coryell system or Walsh's pass-strategy.

Don Coryell coached the San Diego Chargers from 1978 to 1986. He is well known for his innovations to football's passing offense.

Coryell's offense today is commonly known as "Air Coryell". However, the Charger offense lacked the ability to control the clock, resulting in their defense spending too much time on the field. As a result, they fell short of getting to the Super Bowl. He was inducted into the San Diego Chargers Hall of Fame in 1986. Coryell is a member of the College Football Hall of Fame. He did not use a playbook.

Al Saunders was the coach for the Chargers from 1986 to 1988 and became a citizen of the United States in 1960, one of the four foreign-born coaches in the NFL. In college played Defensive Back and Wide Receiver for the Spartans of San Jose State University (SJSU) from 1966 to 1968 where he was a three-year starter, team captain, and an Academic All-American.

In the 1970s, Al Saunders joined the coaching staff at USC and San Diego State University (SDSU), whose SDSU Aztecs were then under the control of Head Coach Don Coryell. Saunders would go with Coryell to NFL when Coryell became the head coach of the San Diego Chargers. Statistics correct as of December 30, 2007, after the end of the 2007 NFL season.

Bobby Ross coached the Chargers from 1992 to 1996, and is the only coach to win awards while coaching the Chargers. In 1992, Ross won the Pro Football Weekly NFL Coach of the Year, the Maxwell Football Club NFL Coach of the Year and the UPI NFL Coach of the Year. The Pro Football Weekly NFL Coach of the Year is presented annually by various news and sports organizations to the National Football

League (NFL) head coach who has done the most outstanding job of working with the talent he has at his disposal. The Maxwell Football Club NFL Coach of the Year was created in 1989 and is originally titled the Earle "Greasy" Neale Award for Professional Coach of the Year. The United Press International (UPI) NFL Coach of the Year award was first presented in 1955. Before the AFL-NFL merger, an award was also given to the most outstanding coach from the AFL. When the leagues merged in 1970, separate awards were given to the best coaches from the AFC and NFC conferences. The UPI discontinued the awards after 1996.

The San Diego Chargers hired Schottenheimer as their 13th head coach on January 29, 2002. Schottenheimer posted a 47–33 record (.588) with the Chargers. His success did not come immediately, as the team posted a 4–12 record in 2003, thereby "earning" the first overall pick in the draft (this was the last time that a team with the worst record in the NFL kept its head coach the following season, even considering the three other 4–12 teams that season replaced their head coaches, Oakland, Arizona, and the New York Giants hiring Norv Turner, Dennis Green, and Tom Coughlin, respectively). He was named NFL Coach Of The Year for the 2004 NFL season. Schottenheimer led the team to two playoff appearances, his 17th and 18th as a head coach. However, both appearances resulted in disappointing losses to the underdog New York Jets in overtime in 2005 and the New England Patriots in 2007, bringing his playoff record to 5–13. Schottenheimer was abruptly fired by San Diego on February 12, 2007. Schottenheimer was fired because of a strained relationship with general manager A.J. Smith, which reached a breaking point when four assistants (Cam

Cameron, Wade Phillips, Rob Chudzinski and Greg Manusky) left for positions with other teams.

There have only been four coaches to lead the team into the playoffs. Bobby Ross holds the best record percentage wise in the playoffs. Norv Turner holds the best regular season coaching record, with 0.640, followed by Hall of Famer Sid Gillman with 0.608. Ron Waller holds the worst regular season record, winning just one out of the six games he coached.

List of Los Angeles Chargers broadcasters

Radio

The Chargers' official flagship station in 2020 is now KYSR 98.7 FM For the previous two seasons, their radio flagship was KFI 640 AM in Los Angeles, commonly known as "KFI AM 640". Chargers daily updates, and specialty shows, will continue to air on FOX Sports 570 KLAC. The broadcast team consists of Play-by-play announcer Matt "Money" Smith and former NFL scout Daniel Jeremiah comprise the broadcast team with KFI morning co-host Shannon Farren serving as sideline reporter. Past Chargers radio broadcasters have included Josh Lewin, Ralph Lawler, Stu Nahan, Tom Kelly, Lee "Hacksaw" Hamilton, Dan Rowe, Ted Leitner, Hank Bauer, and Nick Hardwick. Bauer served seventeen seasons (1998–2014) as the radio color analyst however, the Chargers and then flagship KIOZ decided not to renew his contract, and was replaced by Curtis Conway starting with the 2015 season.

P.A. announcer

Eric Smith the public address announcer of all Clippers basketball games and former Dodgers baseball announcer games, serves as the P.A. announcer of all Charger home games at SoFi Stadium. Smith replaced legendary P.A. announcer Bruce Binkowski, who went on to become the executive director of the Holiday Bowl and Poinsettia Bowl games.

With the Chargers return to Los Angeles in 2017, the team became a beneficiary of league scheduling policies. Both the Chargers and the Los Angeles Rams share the Los Angeles market, which is on the West Coast of the United States. This means that the Chargers cannot play home games, road division games against the Denver Broncos or Oakland Raiders, or interconference road games against the NFC West (in seasons that the AFC West and NFC West meet in interconference play) in the early 10:00 a.m. Pacific time slot. In addition, they cannot play interconference home games at the same time or network as the Rams. As a result, both teams generally will have more limited scheduling options, and will also benefit by receiving more prime-time games than usual. Thus, regardless of the previous season's record, the Chargers will receive a disproportionate number of Sunday Night, Monday Night and/or Thursday Night games, compared to the rest of the league.

Previously when the team was in San Diego its main flagship was KIOZ. The previous Los Angeles flagship was KLAC/570, in Los Angeles and Orange County, which like KIOZ, KLSD, and several other Charger radio affiliates, is owned by iHeartMedia. Prior to that KSPN/710 was the Los Angeles affiliate and before that, KMPC/1540 for several years.

As of 2014, the Chargers also stream their radio broadcasts on their official mobile application (through iOS and Android devices) as well as on their website

Los Angeles Chargers Trivia Questions & Answers

1 The Chargers franchise began it all in the American Football League in 1960. What was their name in that inaugural season?

Answer: Los Angeles Chargers

They played as the Los Angeles Chargers for only one season. They went 10-4 in that first season. In 1961, the franchise was in San Diego under head coach Sid Gillman to help create a fan dynasty.

2 The Chargers had a lot of injured players during the season. Which Charger player attempted to play, but ended up having surgery shortly after playing in one game?

Answer: Shawne Merriman

Shawne Merriman played in the game against Carolina on September 7th. Two days later, he was placed on the injured reserve list. He had surgery on September 15th to repair PCL and LCL tears in his left knee.

3 Which Charger quarterback led the NFL in passing yards in each of the 1979-1982 seasons?

Answer: Dan Fouts

In seasons 1979-1982, Dan Fouts passed for 4082, 4715, 4802, and 2883 respectively. He was a 1973 draft pick out of Oregon and was inducted into the 1993 Pro Football Hall of Fame.

4 What city did the Chargers play their first season in?

Answer: Los Angeles

They played their first season in LA, then moved in 1961 to San Diego. Over the years, the Chargers had hinted that the club might choose to move back to its city of origin.

5 Which Charger quarterback bounced back from a dismal 2003-04 season, winning the Comeback Player of the Year Award, throwing 27 touchdowns to seven interceptions, and landing himself a spot in the 2005 NFL Pro Bowl?

Answer: Drew Brees

Drew Brees made a drastic improvment in 2004. His 65.5% completion percentage improved by almost 8% from 2003. His 3,159 passing yards was over 1,000 more yards than what he threw in 2003. His 27 touchdown passes more than doubled his touchdown passes in 2003. His interceptions went down from 15 to only seven. Brees could do it on the ground too. He had 85 yards rushing and two rushing touchdowns in 2004.

6 Who coached the Chargers to more victories in the 20th century that any other head coach?

Answer: Sid Gillman

Gillman coached the Chargers all the way through the AFL days of the 1960s, except for the last five games of the 1969 season. He then coached them for the first ten games of 1971. He finished his career with a win/loss record of 87-57-6. Don Coryell was second, winning 72 games from 1978-1986.

7 How was the Chargers ranked in defense at the end of the 2002 season?

Answer: 30th

Chargers had one of the most feared defenses prior to the year's defensive debuckle. which is one of the main reasons their main focus on this years draft was on the defensive side of the ball.

8 What position was Quentin Jammer?

Answer: Cornerback

Jammer was the first round draft pick to fill the spot.

9 With 10 seasons under their belt, how many times did the Chargers have a winning record from 1960-1969?

Answer: 9

After their 10-4 record in Los Angeles in the franchise's first season, they went 12-2 the following season and were led by the arm of Jack Kemp. With John Hadl taking snaps in 1962, the team went only 4-10, but Hadl and the team rebounded well. The team merged with the NFL in 1970.

10 Philip Rivers set a Charger record for the most TD passes in a single season. Whose record did he break?

Answer: Dan Fouts

Philip Rivers broke Dan Fouts'record on December 28, 2008, against the Denver Broncos. He threw 2 TD passes that night which gave him 34 TD passes for the season. The previous record was 33 TD passes thrown by Fouts in the 1981 season.

11 Who was the first Charger inducted into the Pro Football Hall of Fame?

Answer: Lance Alworth

Lance Alworth was inducted into the Hall of Fame in 1978 making him the first Charger and the first player to have played in the AFL to be inducted. A 7-time Pro Bowler, his first year out of Arkansas in the big league was in 1962. He played for the Chargers 1962-1970, then the Cowboys 1971-1972.

12 Who was the original owner of the Chargers?

Answer: Barron Hilton

Barron Hilton, of the Hilton Hotels family, was the original owner o the Chargers. Hilton sold the team in 1966 to a group led by Eugene Klein and Sam Schulman.

13 Which Charger Pro Bowl running back rushed for 1,000 yards or more in his fourth consecutive season, and broke the NFL record for most consecutive games with a rushing touchdown in a season?

Answer: LaDainian Tomlinson

LaDainian Tomlinson led the NFL with 17 rushing touchdowns in 2004. LT set a new NFL record in 2004 with a rushing touchdown in 12 consecutive games, breaking the record previously owned by Emmitt Smith and Priest Holmes.

14 Whose single game passing yardage team record did quarterback Dan Fouts tie, when he passed for 444 yards in a 41-37 win over the San Francisco 49ers on December 11, 1982?

Answer: His own

Fouts equalled his own record which he had set two years earlier in a 44-7 win over the New York Giants. At the time of his retirement in 1987, Fouts held many major NFL passing records and virtually every Chargers passing record.

15 Prior to being traded to the Miami Dolphins, Seau had spent many years with the San Diego Chargers. How many of those years had been with the Chargers?

Answer: 13

Seau was a major contributor and role model to the team and to the city of San Diego for thirteen years. No wonder not many fans agreed with this move by the team. Chargers management preach that the move was strictly business.

16 Who was the Chargers backup quarterback?

Answer: Doug Flutie

Brees topped Flutie in the pre-season.

17 In which season did the Chargers make the team's first playof appearance?

Answer: 1960

With their 10-4 record, the Chargers won the AFL West Division They lost the championship game to the Houston Oilers 24-16.

18 Which player led the team in the number of receiving yards?

Answer: Vincent Jackson

Vincent Jackson had 59 receptions for 1098 yards. He scored 7 receiving touchdowns as well. Antonio Gates was second on the team with 60 catches for 704 yards. Malcolm Floyd had 27 catches for 465 yards.

19 A Pro Bowl defensive end, which player was traded mid-season in 1981 to the San Francisco 49ers and went on to be voted NFC Player of the Year in that same season?

Answer: Fred Dean

Fred Dean came out of Louisiana Tech in 1975. He played for the Chargers 1975-1981, then was traded to the 1981 Super Bowl Champion San Francisco 49ers after a few games into the 1981 season.

He finished his career with the 49ers after the 1985 season. He was voted NFC Player of the Year in 1981. He was a 4-time Pro Bowler and was elected to the Pro Football Hall of Fame in February 2008.

20 After moving to San Diego, what stadium did the Chargers call home?

Answer: Balboa Stadium

After playing their first season in LA at Los Angeles Memorial Coliseum, the Chargers moved to San Diego and played six seasons in Balboa Stadium.

21 What college did Dan Fouts attend?

Answer: Oregon

He threw for 5995 yards in his college career and was drafted in the 3rd round. Although not expected to become a superstar, Fouts eventually would set many NFL records (later passed by the likes of Marino, Favre, and Elway).

22 This Charger tight end according to many, was the best tight end in 2004 and was perhaps the biggest bargain in years. He set a NFL record that year for most touchdowns scored by a tight end in a season with 13. Who was this Pro Bowl tight end?

Answer: Antonio Gates

Antonio Gates earned his first Pro-Bowl selection in the 2004-0!
season. That season, he set a new NFL record with 13 touchdowns b
a tight end in a single season. In 2004-05, Gates caught 81 passes fo
964 receiving yards; averaging about 12 yards per reception.

23 How many times was Seau voted to attend the Pro Bowl as ;
Charger?

Answer: 13

24 Who was the Chargers' first running back to rush for 1000 yards ir
a season?

Answer: Paul Lowe

The two-time Pro Bowler rushed for 1010 yards in 1963, and anothe:
1121 yards in 1965. Former USC star Mike Garrett would be the nex:
with 1031 yards in 1972 to surpass the 1000-yard season milestone. Ir
2001, LaDainian Tomlinson was a Charger rookie, and rushed for 123€
yards.

26 Ed Hoculi made a error judgment call that went against the
Chargers in week 2. What team benefited from the call and won the
game as a result?

Answer: Denver Broncos

Denver quarterback Jay Cutler dropped back for a pass. The ball slipped out of his hands and Chargers linebacker, Tim Dobbins, had recoved the football. The play was ruled dead when Ed Hoculi blew the whistle too soon. As a result, the Broncos retained possession and ended up winning the game.

27 Which former Charger wide receiver out of Grambling State was inducted into the Pro Football Hall of Fame in 1996?

Answer: Charlie Joiner

An 18-year veteran, Charlie Joiner played with the Houston Oilers 1969-1972, Cincinnati Bengals 1972-1975 and the Chargers 1976-1986. He was a 3-time Pro Bowler as a Charger.

28 Who was the first coach of the Chargers?

Answer: Sid Gilman

Sid Gilman coached the Chargers 1960-1969. He was inducted into the Pro Football Hall of Fame in 1983.

29 How many players did the Chargers draft in the first round in the 1990s?

Answer: 5

They drafted Junior Seau(90), Stanley Richard(91), Chris Mims(92), Darrien Gordon(93), and Ryan Leaf(98). Bobby Beathard didn't believe in building through first round picks, but he had a "sure thing" in 1998 that he couldn't pass up. In fact, the Chargers were slated to pick 3rd in the 1998 draft, but traded up one spot with the Arizona Cardinals (giving the Cards their following season's first round pick and much more).

30 Perhaps one of the most underrated players in football, this Charger fullback had paved the way for numerous 1,000 yard rushers including Eddie George and Corey Dillion. In 2004, he did it for LaDainian Tonlinson. Who was this overlooked fullback?

Answer: Lorenzo Neal

With every great running back there is a great fullback blocking for him. That was the case in 2004 when Lorenzo Neal paved the way for 1,000 yard rusher, LaDainian Tomlinson. Neal had a streak of blocking for 1,000 yard rushers from 1997 and continued in 2004.

31 Along with Seau, which Charger Pro Bowl safety was not in a Chargers uniform in 2002?

Answer: Rodney Harrison

Was one of my favorite players in the entire league. Was nicknamed "The Hitman" because of his outstanding ability to but the hurt on anyone with the ball.

32 For which season did the Chargers make their first Super Bowl appearance?

Answer: 1994

The 1994 Chargers were helmed by Bobby Ross, and finished the season with a respectable 11-5 record. They won the AFC West by two games over the Chiefs, then went on to win the Division Championship over the Dolphins, 22-21. Then they won in another squeaker by topping the Steelers 17-13 in the Conference Championship. The Chargers were stopped in a big way in Super Bowl XXIX, 49-26, at the hands of the San Francisco 49ers.

33 Which San Diego offensive lineman was nicknamed, "The Intellectual Assassin"?

Answer: Ron Mix

Ron Mix received a Juris Doctor degree from USC, thus received his nickname. An original Charger, he played 1960-1969 with San Diego, and 1971 with the Oakland Raiders. He was called for only two holding penalties in ten seasons. Mix was inducted into the Pro Football Hall of Fame in 1979.

34 In the Chargers first six AFL seasons, how many AFL Championship appearances did they make?

Answer: 5

The Chargers went to the AFL Championship in all but one season o their first six. They won the 1963 AFL Championship.

35 Who was the first coach to lead the Chargers to a Super Bowl?

Answer: Bobby Ross

After winning a National Championship at Georgia Tech, Ross took over a team that had gone 22-42 the previous 4 seasons. He is possibly the most successful coach in team history. In his five seasons, the team didn't have one year with a losing record. He also owned a respectable 3-3 mark in the playoffs.

36 Which wide receiver led the San Diego Chargers in 2004 with 47 receptions?

Answer: Eric Parker

The Chargers were anchored by wide receivers Eric Parker and Reche Caldwell early in the season, but when Caldwell went down with injury, all the Chargers did was sign Pro Bowl wideout Keenan McCardell from Tampa Bay, to propel them the rest of the way.

37 Which team did the Chargers defeat for their first postseason win after the 1970 NFL/AFL merger?

Answer: Buffalo Bills

The Chargers beat the Bills 20-14 in a 1980 AFC divisional playoff game to advance to the AFC Championship Game, where they lost 34-27 to the Oakland Raiders.

38 Lorenzo Neal, a new Pro Bowl full back acquired by the Chargers from what team?

Answer: Cincinnati Bengals

After releasing 13 year veteran Fred McCrary, the Chargers signed Lorenzo Neal to be the lead blocker for Ladanian Tomlinson.

39 Who did Marty Schotenheimer replace in 2002?

Answer: Mike Riley

Marty Schotenheimer is the new coach who seems to be the solution.

40 Who was the first Charger kicker to score 100 points in a season for the team?

Answer: Dennis Partee

In 1968 when Partee was a rookie Charger, he booted 106 points for the team in the season. It would be the only time that Dennis would top the 100-point mark. He retired in 1974 from the NFL after only six seasons.

41 Who did the Chargers defeat in the wildcard game on Saturday January 3rd?

Answer: Indianapolis Colts

The Chargers defeated the Colts 23-17 in overtime. Darren Sproles scored the game-winning touchdown.

42 Which Charger was the first tight end to lead the league in receptions in back to back seasons 1980 and 1981?

Answer: Kellen Winslow

Kellen Winslow was drafted out of Missouri in 1979 and played his entire career with the Chargers until 1987. He had 89 receptions in 1980 and 88 in 1981 to the lead the league in back to back seasons. He was inducted into the Pro Football Hall of Fame in 1995.

43 Who did the Chargers defeat when they won the 1963 AFL Championship game?

Answer: Boston Patriots

The 1963 AFL Championship was played in Balboa Stadium in San Diego on January 5, 1964. The San Diego Chargers defeated the Boston Patriots 51-10.

44 What Charger led the NFL in receiving yards (1340) and TDs (13) in 1980?

Answer: John Jefferson

"JJ" also had an excellent SI photo cover that year. For some reason, the Chargers got rid of him the next year and he never put up similar numbers with Green Bay. Wes Chandler would help fans forget JJ, however no old-timer fan can forget the contribution he made to winning in the late 1970s and early 1980s.

45 In 2004, which AFC West opponent did the San Diego Chargers beat twice, to sweep them in the season series for the first time since 1992?

Answer: Oakland Raiders

The San Diego Chargers clobbered the Oakland Raiders 42-14 in thei first meeting on Halloween day 2004 in San Diego. Then three week later the Chargers went in the Black Hole and came out with anothe victory, as they beat the Raiders 23-17 to sweep them in a season serie for the first time in a dozen years.

46 Which team did the Chargers defeat in the 1994 AFC Championship Game to advance to Super Bowl XXIX?

Answer: Pittsburgh Steelers

The Chargers, under head coach Bobby Ross, stunned the Steelers ir Pittsburgh 17-13. They then lost Super Bowl XXIX 49-26 to the Sar Francisco 49ers.

47 Who were the Chargers' opponents in the second round (AFC Divisional) of the 2008 season playoffs?

Answer: Pittsburgh Steelers

They lost to the Steelers 35-24. The Pittsburgh defense played solid throughout the game. The Chargers' offense had possession of the football for only 17 seconds in the third quarter of the game.

48 What Charger quarterback led the team to the upset win of the AFC Championship vs the Pittsburgh Steelers in the 1994 season?

Answer: Stan Humphries

On the way to their first Super Bowl, the Chargers beat the Dan Marino led Dolphins in the Divisional Playoffs and then upset the Pittsburgh Steelers at Three Rivers Stadium for the Conference Championship title. They lost to the San Francisco 49ers in Super Bowl XXIX. Humphries was the San Diego offensive leader. He played for the Redskins 1989-1991, the Chargers 1992-1997 then retired after having several concussions.

49 Who was voted NFL MVP for the strike-shortened 1982 season?

Answer: Dan Fouts

Fouts played his entire professional career with the Chargers from 1973-1987. Not only was Dan Fouts voted 1982 NFL MVP, but also Pro Bowl MVP and Offensive Player of the Year. He was inducted into the Pro Football Hall of Fame in 1993.

51 Which Charger somersaulted the Dolphin defense into the endzone during the season opening 50-26 victory at home in 1986?

Answer: Gary Anderson

One of the great Charger highlights of all-time. Unfortunately, the Chargers finished the season 4-12, and Anderson rushed for only 445 yards. Gary Anderson, a former first round pick, also caught 80 passes for 871 yards with 8 touchdowns that season. The 1986 season also was the end of an era, as Don Coryell exited unceremoniously after starting the season 1-7.

52 The Chargers had one shutout victory in the postseason during th 20th century. Which team was the unfortunate victim?

Answer: Kansas City Chiefs

The Chargers blanked the Chiefs 17-0 in one of the 1992 AFC Wildcard Games. Unfortunately for the Chargers, their season ended a week later with a 31-0 loss to the Miami Dolphins.

53 Who was the first Charger in the team's history to have good enough hands for 100 receptions in a season?

Answer: LaDainian Tomlinson

The others were great, but never had more than 75 receptions in a season for San Diego. Tomlinson hit the century mark in 2003 in his third season with the Chargers. From the ground in 2003, LaDainiar scored 13 rushing touchdowns, and with 100 receptions he scored only four from the air.

54 Two Chargers were named to the Pro Bowl for 2008. Kris Dielman an offensive guard was one of them. Who was the other?

Answer: Antonio Gates

Antonio Gates was selected to his 5th straight Pro Bowl. Surprisingly, Philip Rivers was not named to the Pro Bowl team despite leading the NFL in passing rating, and tying with Drew Brees (Saints) for the most TD passes thrown (34).

55 In order to insure getting one of two quarterbacks in the 1998 draft, which Chargers pick was deemed worthy of trading two first-round picks, a second-round pick, linebacker Patrick Sapp and Pro Bowler Eric Metcalf?

Answer: Ryan Leaf

The two quarterbacks that were considered to be the best in the 1998 draft were Peyton Manning and Ryan Leaf. Other notable quarterbacks in that draft were Matt Hasselback and Brian Griese. The Colts took Manning as the first overall pick and the Chargers took Leaf. Leaf is considered one of the biggest flops in NFL history. His rookie sign-on bonus was the largest for a rookie at that time. He lasted with the Chargers 1998-2000, sitting out the entire 1999 season due to injury. He was traded to the Bucs after the 2000 season, then to Dallas the same year. He finished his NFL career in 2002 with the Seahawks offseason and practice squad. Despite poor game performances with San Diego he was noted to have poor team and media realtions as well.

56 Which Chargers coach was voted AFC Coach of the Year for the 1992 season?

Answer: Bobby Ross

The Chargers finished the 1991 season 4-12 under Dan Henning. Th 1992 season saw a turn-around under the direction of Bobby Ross The team finished the regular season 11-5, went to the playoffs an eventually lost the divisional title to the Dolphins.

57 A memorable season opener in 1994 featured Junior Seau playing the game with one arm in a cast, and grabbing a late 4th quarte interception to clinch a 37-34 win. Which AFC West foe did th Chargers beat on the road that night?

Answer: Denver Broncos

A tough win in Denver that night was a catalyst for this team's 6-0 star and eventual Super Bowl run. It was one of the greatest game Junio ever played, and nobody would ever question the man's toughnes after this gritty performance.

58 2002 did not see John Parella in a Charger uniform. Which team did go to?

Answer: Oakland Raiders

He is on the Defensive Line, wore #97 and went to the Raiders.

59 In the 2008 season, the Chargers limped to a record of 8-8, but was good enough to win the AFC West. After defeating the Colts in the wildcard game 23-17, which team stopped the Chargers in the Division Championship game?

Answer: Pittsburgh Steelers

Ben Roethlisberger and the Steelers stopped the Chargers in their tracks, 35-24. The Steelers would go all the way to win the Super Bowl against the Cardinals, 27-23.

60 Which San Diego linebacker was nicknamed the "Tasmanian Devil"?

Answer: Junior Seau

Junior Seau was a first round draft pick by the Chargers out of Southern California. He played with the Chargers 1990-2002, then off to Miami for three seasons before ending up in New England. He led the team in tackles each of his seasons with the Chargers. He was a 12-time Pro Bowler 1991-2002 including all his Charger seasons except his rookie year.

61 Who did the Chargers play in Super Bowl XXIX?

Answer: San Francisco 49ers

Super Bowl XXIX was played January 29, 1995, in Miami at Joe Robbi Stadium. The Chargers lost to the 49ers 49-26, a sad ending to successful 1994 season.

62 After starting 0-4 in 1992, the Chargers finished 11-5 to win th AFC West. Which divisional foe did the Chargers beat 17-0 in th wildcard game?

Answer: Kansas City Chiefs

The highlight was Marion Butts' 54-yard TD run. Unfortuately, th Chargers lost the next game 31-0 on a sad, rainy day in Miami. Th team would get a certain level of payback two years later in memorable 22-21 victory over the Dolphins.

63 Perhaps the most vital part of 2004 was the rapid improvement o the Charger defense. A defense that ranked third in points allowed anc third in rushing defense. Which premier defender led the Chargers ir tackles with 151?

Answer: Donnie Edwards

Donnie Edwards had a career season in 2004 with 151 tackles, five interceptions, eight pass deflections, and one touchdown. Edward: was one of the biggest Pro Bowl snubs. Other notable defender: include another Pro Bowl snub, Jamal Williams, along with Terrance

Kiel, Steve Foley, Randall Godfrey, and Jerry Wilson, who all had nothing short of a great season.

64 Which college did Chargers running back LaDainian Tomlinson attend?

Answer: Texas Christian

Tomlinson quickly became one of the best running backs in the NFL. Chargers head coach Marty Schottenheimer said Tomlinson was the greatest running back he's ever seen play.

5 Curtis Conway was what number?

Answer: 80

Curtis Conway was the leading receiver on the Chargers.

66 In 2006, the Chargers had an exceptional season by going 14-2. The team was led by the arm of Philip Rivers, the legs of running back LaDainian Tomlinson, and which head coach?

Answer: Marty Schottenheimer

The Charger fans had their hopes high after a spectacular season, but lost the Division Championship to the Patriots, 24-21. Schottenheimer was in his fifth season at the helm of the Chargers, and the relationship between the upper brass and Schottenheimer was terminated after that loss.

67 Who led the team in interceptions?

Answer: Stephen Cooper

Linebacker Stephen Cooper had four interceptions. Cason, Jammer and Cromartie each had 2 interceptions. Cason and Cromartie each ran back an interception for a touchdown.

68 Which Charger was the NFL MVP Award winner for the 2006 season?

Answer: LaDainian Tomlinson

LaDainian "LT" Tomlinson was a first round draft pick out of Texas Christian in the 2001 draft. He's a San Diego fan favorite. In each of his first seven seasons he rushed for over 1200 yards and had over 50 receptions. In 2003, he was the first NFL player to rush for over 1000 yards and have over 100 catches in the same season!

69 Who was the tight end out of Missouri chosen by the Chargers in the first round of the 1979 NFL Draft?

Answer: Kellen Winslow

Kellen played his entire professional career with the Chargers 1979-1987. He was a 5-time Pro Bowl selection and was inducted to the Pro Football Hall of Fame in 1995.

70 19 games, 3160 yards, 14 TDs, 29 INTs, and a 52.4 QB rating. Which Charger QB of the 1990s did these career statistics belong to as a Charger?

Answer: Craig Whelihan

Sadly, all these quarterbacks started during the late 1990s, and those teams combined for a 23-57 record. Moses Moreno only played in 6 games. Erik Kramer threw 2 TDs and 10 INT in 1999 then retired. Ryan Leaf threw for 13 TD and 33 INT during his 3-year stint in San Diego.

71 Who were the 2004 AFC West Division Champions?

Answer: San Diego Chargers

The 2004 San Diego Chargers ended the regular season with a 12-4 record and were the 2004 AFC West Division Champions. Led by coach Marty Schottenheimer, the famous 'Martyball' rode the San Diego Chargers all the way into the postseason. The 2004 San Diego Chargers were a team to remember. Let's admit it, in 2004 we were all "shocked by the "Bolt"!

72 Whose team record did LaDainian Tomlinson break when h rushed for 1,683 yards in 2002?

Answer: Natrone Means

Means' 1,350 yards set a team record in 1994.

73 Who was nicknamed L.T.?

Answer: LaDainian Tomlinson

LaDainian Tomlinson was a leading rusher.

Made in the USA
Middletown, DE
22 February 2023

25379427R00035